Extreme Cuisine
Mammal Menu

by Meish Goldish

Consultants:
David George Gordon, author of *The Eat-a-Bug Cookbook*
Andrew Zimmern, co-creator and host of *Bizarre Foods with Andrew Zimmern*

BEARPORT
PUBLISHING

New York, New York

Credits

Cover and Title Page, © Suzannah Skelton/iStockphoto and Tatiana Morozova/Shutterstock; 4, © Mikael Damkier/Shutterstock; 5, © Jason A. Holechek, 2008; 6T, © Barry Bland/Alamy; 6B, © PetStockBoys/Alamy; 7, © Michael Freeman/Corbis; 8, © Tamsin Eyles/www.tamsineyles.co.uk; 9, © Franck Bichon Photographe; 10, © Top-Pics TBK/Alamy; 11, © FabFoodPix/StockFood; 12, © Mwizenge S. Tembo; 13, © Mwizenge S. Tembo; 14, © Massimo Casal/CasalPhotography; 15, © Massimo Casal/CasalPhotography; 16, © JTB Photo Communications, Inc./Alamy; 17, © Richard Prudhomme/editorial stock photography; 18, © Pichugin Dmitry/Shutterstock; 19, © Matthew Choy; 20, © Anatoli Dubkov/Shutterstock; 21, © John Tong; 23TL, © Pichugin Dmitry/Shutterstock; 23TR, © Sebastian Kaulitzki/Shutterstock; 23BL, © Anatoli Dubkov/Shutterstock; 23BR, © Pascal Goetgheluck/Photo Researchers, Inc.

Publisher: Kenn Goin
Editorial Director: Adam Siegel
Creative Director: Spencer Brinker
Design: Debrah Kaiser
Photo Researcher: Nancy Tobin

Library of Congress Cataloging-in-Publication Data

Goldish, Meish.
  Mammal menu / by Meish Goldish.
      p. cm. — (Extreme cuisine)
  Includes bibliographical references and index.
  ISBN-13: 978-1-59716-760-4 (lib. binding)
  ISBN-10: 1-59716-760-6 (lib. binding)
  1. Cookery (Meat)—Juvenile literature. 2. Mammals—Juvenile literature. 3. Cookery, International—Juvenile literature. I. Title.

  TX749.G55 2009
  641.6'6—dc22

                          2008034876

For more information, write to Bearport Publishing Company, Inc., 101 Fifth Avenue, Suite 6R, New York, New York 10003. Printed in the United States of America.

10 9 8 7 6 5 4 3 2 1

MENU

Grilled Cow's Heart

Cooks around the world make delicious dishes using meat from cows, sheep, pigs, and other **mammals**. For example, hamburgers are made using ground meat from cows. In Peru, some people use cow's heart to make a tasty meal. Why not? It's part of a cow, too! To make this dish, the cook chops the heart into pieces and adds hot sauce. The meat is then cooked on a grill. It is usually served with potatoes or corn. Now that's a "hearty" meal!

About 4,000 kinds of animals are mammals.

cow's heart

Fried Bat

Bats are the only mammals that fly. Yet that hasn't stopped some people in Thailand from catching them. Villagers simply place a net outside the entrance to the bats' cave. When the furry fliers leave their home in search of food, they get trapped. Soon they are turned into a crispy treat.

Before bats are cooked, their hair needs to be removed. Some people burn it off. Others skin the bat. The animal is then cut into small chunks. To prepare the dish, villagers grill or fry the bite-sized pieces with salt, pepper, garlic, and onions. Many people say bat meat tastes a lot like chicken.

When a bat is small, people sometimes eat the whole animal—including the head, crunchy bones, and wings.

fried bat

Pig's Blood Pudding

Barbecued spareribs, pork chops, and bacon are all made using meat from a pig. Yet meat isn't the only part of a pig that some people eat. On the island of Trinidad, pig's blood is used to make a kind of sausage called black pudding. The blood is mixed with bread crumbs and rice and stuffed into a piece of pig's **intestine**. The sausages are then cooked in hot water until they become firm.

Black pudding is also eaten in many European countries, including England, Scotland, France, Spain, and Germany. Each place makes it in a slightly different way and may call it by a different name. Yet it always has one thing in common—pig's blood.

Black pudding is sometimes called blood pudding.

blood pudding

Stuffed Sheep

Sheep's wool is used to knit sweaters, socks, and mittens. In Scotland, a sheep's heart, liver, and lungs are boiled to make a dish called haggis (HAG-iss). After the body parts are boiled, they are chopped up and mixed with oatmeal, onions, and seasonings. Then it's all stuffed inside a sheep's stomach and boiled for about three hours. Often served with potatoes, haggis has been enjoyed by people in Scotland for hundreds of years.

haggis

Haggis hurling is a sport in Scotland. Players see who can throw a frozen haggis the farthest. The current record is 180 feet and 10 inches (55 m and 25 cm).

Mouse Meals

Many people are afraid of mice—but not in parts of Zambia (ZAM-bee-uh). Men and boys in the eastern part of this African country hunt the little wild mammals for food. They dig for mice in the holes in the ground where they live. When the small animals run out of their homes to find a safer place to hide, the hunters catch them.

To prepare the mice, villagers first remove the animals' insides. Next, they boil the mice in water and add salt. The small animals are then dried by the fire. They are now ready to be eaten with *nshima*—a thick cornmeal dish that people in Zambia eat each day for lunch and dinner.

Mice can be healthful to eat. They are a good source of protein, which the human body uses to build bone and muscle.

13

Dog Dishes

In most countries, dogs make great pets. In some places, however, they make a tasty meal. In parts of Vietnam, dog meat is used to make many different dishes. Some people grill the meat. Others stir-fry thin slices of dog tongue with garlic and vegetables. Dog soup, made with bamboo **shoots**, is also served in restaurants. Some people in Vietnam believe that eating the soup will make them healthy and lucky.

dog meat

Some people in China, Thailand, and Korea also eat dog meat.

grilled dog meat

Raw Horse Meatballs

Most meatballs are made from ground beef or pork. In France, however, they're also made from ground horse meat—and that's not the only difference. They're also eaten raw. Whoa! Now that's some dish.

It's very simple to make horse meatballs. Just add one egg, garlic, salt, and pepper to the ground meat. Then shape it into balls. Some people place chopped onions around the meatballs and serve them with ketchup, olive oil, and soy sauce. The meat isn't just tasty, it's healthful, too. Horse meat has fewer calories than lean beef. Maybe that's why cooks in Japan, Belgium, and Sweden also make dishes using raw horse meat.

horse meatballs

It is not always safe
to eat raw meat and eggs.
For example, raw meat that
has been left out of the
refrigerator too long
can go bad.

Camel Cuisine

Camels have wide, soft feet that help them walk in the sand. In parts of China, those feet are also a treat to eat. Some people turn them into a delicious paste. First, they remove the hair and bone from each foot. Then they cook the foot pads with spices. It turns into a thick paste. People use this paste to make a soup-like dish that also includes scallops, mushrooms, and ham.

Feet aren't the only part of a camel that people eat. The meat in camels' **humps** is also popular. It is usually roasted. Many say it is the tastiest part of the animal.

hump

camel hump meat

In Mongolia,
the fat from a camel's
hump is used to
make butter.

Squirrel: Grilled, Stewed, or Scrambled

In the United States, the mammals most often eaten are cows, pigs, and sheep. In Kentucky and other southern states, however, some people eat another kind of mammal—squirrel. Sometimes cooks grill squirrel meat or use it to make a stew. Other times people just eat the animal's brains!

How are squirrel brains prepared? First, the animal's head is shaved. Then it is fried and cracked open. The brains inside are now ready to be sucked out. Some people prepare squirrel brains in a different way. They scramble them in gravy or with eggs. People don't get smarter by eating mammal brains, but they do have a meal they will never forget.

Doctors warn people not to eat squirrel brains because the animals may carry a deadly disease.

grilled squirrel

Where Are They Eaten?

Here are some of the places where
the mammal meals in this book are eaten.

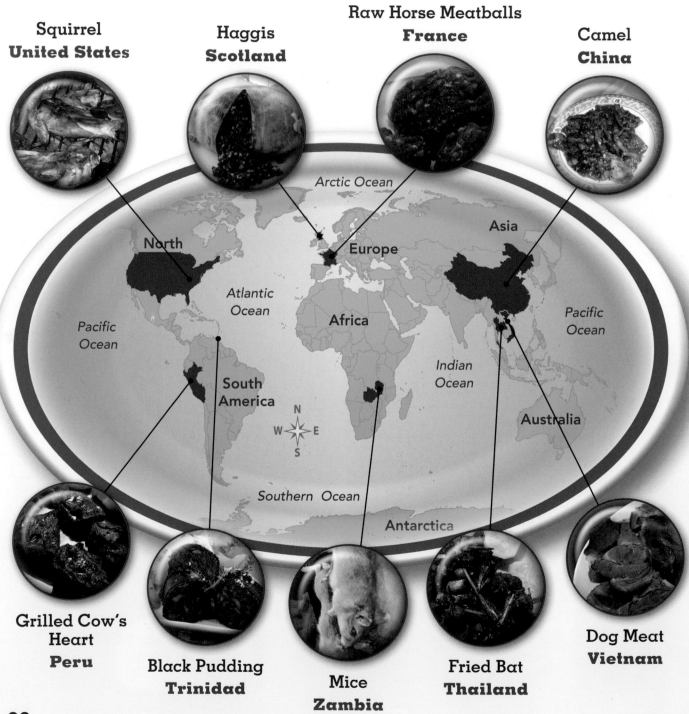

Squirrel
United States

Haggis
Scotland

Raw Horse Meatballs
France

Camel
China

Arctic Ocean

North

Europe

Asia

Atlantic
Ocean

Africa

Pacific
Ocean

Pacific
Ocean

South
America

Indian
Ocean

N
W ✴ E
S

Australia

Southern Ocean

Antarctica

Grilled Cow's
Heart
Peru

Black Pudding
Trinidad

Mice
Zambia

Fried Bat
Thailand

Dog Meat
Vietnam

Glossary

humps (HUHMPS)
the large lumps on
camels' backs where
the animals store fat

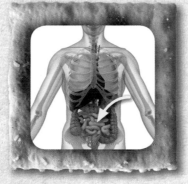

intestine (in-TESS-tin)
a long tube inside a
mammal's belly that
helps break down food

mammals (MAM-uhlz)
warm-blooded animals that
have a backbone and hair
or fur on their skin; they
also drink their mothers'
milk as babies

shoots (SHOOTS)
the new parts of a
plant that are just
starting to grow

Index

Bibliography

Hopkins, Jerry. *Extreme Cuisine: The Weird & Wonderful Foods That People Eat.* London: Bloomsbury (2004).

Schwabe, Calvin W. *Unmentionable Cuisine.* Charlottesville, VA: University Press of Virginia (1994).

Read More

Miller, Connie Colwell. *Disgusting Foods.* Mankato, MN: Capstone Press (2007).

Solheim, James. *It's Disgusting and We Ate It!: True Food Facts from Around the World and Throughout History.* New York: Simon & Schuster (2001).

Wishinsky, Frieda, and Elizabeth MacLeod. *Everything but the Kitchen Sink: Weird Stuff You Didn't Know About Food.* New York: Scholastic (2008).

Learn More Online

To learn more about unusual mammal dishes, visit
www.bearportpublishing.com/ExtremeCuisine

About the Author

Meish Goldish has written more than 100 books for children.
He lives in Brooklyn, New York.